Time Bring About a Change

Time Bring About a Change

A memoir by
Tony Carr

Mill City Press, Inc.
212 3rd Avenue North, Suite 290
Minneapolis, MN 55401
612.455.2294
www.millcitypublishing.com

ISBN-13: 978-1-937600-51-8
LCCN: 2011943236

Cover Design by Mill City Press Design Team
Typeset by Wendy Baker

Printed in the United States of America

Dedication

This book is dedicated to Francesca, Gionna, Eden, and Carmen. All I ask is that you keep the family legacy alive and be true to the values of your ancestors. Be proud of who you are and never feel that you are inferior to anyone. Always remember to treat people the way you want to be treated. Remember that you are sisters and always love and watch over one another.

I thank you, Amy, for choosing me as your husband and for standing by my side through the challenges and struggles. I thank you for being a loving wife and a wonderful and spiritual mother to our children.

I thank all of my family for the love and support you have always given me. You have always been there to pick me up when I am down or bring me back to earth when my head was way above the clouds. Thank you for keeping me humble.

I thank all the people, too many to mention, who have touched my life in both positive and negative ways. I have learned many lessons from them all.

I thank God for putting me on this journey, for through Him all things are possible. I will continue this journey by faith and purpose, and I cherish the spirit that guides and lives in me.

Foreword

This book was written first and foremost in honor and memory of my grandparents and parents and countless others in our nations history who faced injustices and dehumanization while not having the voice or support to speak up for what was right. The struggles of the past should never be forgotten; we must understand our past to create a better future.

We as a society have become more tolerant, but we still have many obstacles to overcome. We must unite to ensure a brighter tomorrow for our children and their children. The chain of generational ignorance and racism must be broken. Rather than be divided by race, we must become simply the human race.

Some people may find it difficult to change their prejudices—and the truth is, we all have them—but I challenge people to just try to become more sensitive to people's differences and to think carefully before speaking. If more of us would put those two simple actions into practice, our society would be on the way to becoming far more positive and unified. The title of my book comes from a hope expressed by my grandfather. I heard him say many times from my youth into my adult years: "Time bring about a change."

Peace,
Tony Carr

Chapter One
Coming of Age

It was a very hot July day in 1969 when my mother said she had something important to tell me. What she shared with me on that day would change my life.

I grew up in Beloit, Wisconsin, a small industrial city in the southern part of the state. My neighborhood was predominantly African American, but there were whites that lived in our community, too. I can remember looking out my bedroom window at the nearby railroad tracks and waving at hoboes who caught a ride on the back of a slow-moving train car. It may not have been the greatest neighborhood, but for me, it was a fascinating place to grow up. My family was loving and compassionate. I was fortunate and blessed to have both my mom and dad at home, along with my older brother. My grandparents and aunt lived just three blocks away on the other side of the railroad tracks.

The late 1960s were a time of turmoil and change in America, and I remember that during my childhood, the television news was full of protests and riots, civil rights demonstrations and reports of the Vietnam War. That was a lot for a young boy to take in. But none of it had really touched me personally—until that day in July of 1969, when I was nine years old.

My mother told me she had received a letter from the school district notifying her that in August I would have to attend a new elementary school. I didn't understand. I loved my school, Burdge Elementary. It was only two blocks from our house, and all my friends were there. The new school that I was to attend, Royce Elementary, was at least a mile away. I wouldn't know anyone there. There was something else about the new school that would be different: Royce was an all-white school. All my friends at Burdge looked like me—black.

I thought my mom was joking.

"Are we moving?" I asked.

She replied no.

"Why do I have to go to a new school?"

My mother tried to explain that it was due to re-zoning of the school district. The re-zoning did not affect my older brother because he was at the junior high where all students from the school district went. I didn't understand that at the time, but when I look back now, I believe that I was a part of an integration mandate. President Lyndon B. Johnson signed the Civil Rights Act in 1964, which made racial discrimination in public places illegal. Supreme Court rulings between 1965–1971 made it clear that schools must desegregate. In many cities the desegregation was being accomplished through court-ordered re-zoning and forced busing.

So many emotions went through me. I was sad, angry, and scared of the unknown. I couldn't imagine having to leave all my friends. I told my mother that I was going to take a knife and kill myself if I had to go to Royce. That was when my mother and grandparents sat me down and gave me a serious lesson about life. They explained how throughout American history, black people had been treated unfairly because of the color of our skin. In the South, all aspects of life were segregated by law. Blacks and whites were not allowed to eat in the same restaurants, attend the same schools, or even drink out of the same water fountains. The recent events of the civil rights movement had brought about change, but it was a slow and painful struggle. My mother and grandparents, who were from small towns in Mississippi, had experienced this racism firsthand.

My mother went to a colored-only school in Mississippi, and although she learned the basics, the education standards and school supplies were far inferior to those of the white schools. In her small one-room school there were children of different ages. My grandparents' educational opportunities were even bleaker. Like many black people in the South at that time, they were sharecroppers—poor farmers who grew their crops on someone else's land. Sharecroppers had to give part of their crop every year to pay their rent, which meant they were rarely able to save any money, and had to work hard to survive. The children in sharecropping families rarely got any education. They were needed to work on the farm, and had no time for school. As a result my grandmother went to school up to the seventh grade, but my grandfather never mentioned attending any school.

My mother and grandparents verbally painted a picture of how going to this new school was going to take my way of thinking and learning to a new level. They encouraged me to take advantage of this opportunity that they were never afforded. Eventually, I realized I did not have a choice.

The First Day

The rest of that summer of 1969 went too quickly, and before I knew it, I was walking through the doors at Royce Elementary. Gathering my courage, I glanced around at the other children. My heart leapt into my throat: No one looked like me.

I was welcomed into the classroom by my fourth-grade teacher, Mrs. Higgins, a very tall white lady with jet-black hair. Mrs. Higgins introduced me to my class and explained that I came from another school. After the introduction there was a dead silence—everyone was staring at me as though I were a zoo animal. Then the whispering started. I tried to block out the whispers and remember what my grandfather had told me: "You put your pants on the same way everyone else does, and there is no one that is any better than you. You get what you came there for, an education." My grandfather was great at phrasing words that kept me focused and motivated.

I initially dreaded going to recess and lunch. I just wanted to get through my classes and go home, never to return again. However, I knew that was not going to happen. Like it or not, I would have to mingle and try to assimilate into this new school environment. I also understood that it was just a matter of time before racial names would come to the surface. Well, it didn't take long enough. I was called names like nigger lips, spear chucker, spook, and a host of other degrading descriptors. My parents had taught me that if someone punched me, I could punch them back—but I should never start a fight over someone's words. So, I took the name-calling and just let the anger build up inside of me.

A Challenge

Three weeks into the school year, things started to change. One day at recess, I was standing by the basketball court when a sixth grader approached me and challenged me to a game of one-on-one. Now, this sixth-grade boy was probably one of the most popular kids in the school. I happily accepted his challenge, for I was fortunate to have been blessed with athleticism and the ability to play basketball at an early age. My mom's brother, Uncle Everett, had played with the Harlem Globetrotters and Harlem Magicians in the late 1950s and early '60s, and in the 1970s he had started his own team called the Broadway Clowns. When I was five years old, he began teaching me the fine art of basketball fundamentals and showmanship.

Uncle Everett was not only a mentor to me athletically, but socially as well.

But I probably give my brother, Steve, the most credit for my basketball abilities. I always wanted to beat him, and he would never let me. Steve gave me no special treatment, and he was very hard on me when we played basketball. There were times when I hated him for it, but when I look back now, I realize that all those years of playing with my brother helped make me both mentally and physically tough.

When I was five, my father and grandfather cut out a backboard made of wood, added a wooden pole, cemented it into the ground, and, after attaching a rim and net to the pre-cut wooden backboard, we had a basketball court. Playing on that makeshift basketball court into the darkness of night were some of the happiest times of my life. The game would consist of Uncle Everett and me against my father and brother and cousin Kim. Uncle Everett and I would always win because he did all the hard work and created wide-open shots for me.

SWISH

Three Years Old And Shy As Can Be
All Confused, But There's Love In The Family
My Teddy Bear (Brownie) Is My Only Friend
Mom Is Always With Me From Beginning To The End

Started In An Urban School
Yeah, It's Mostly Black
School Board Votes Integration
White School Says Go Back

Confusion Is Back Again
White Children Call Me Names
Do They Really Hate My Race?
Or Are Their Parents To Blame?

I Became A Loner
Finding Peace Within My Space
Learning One Thing Daily
That It's A Cold, Cold Human Race

But I Came Across A Basketball
Not Trusting Anyone
Uncle, Dad, And My Brother
Showed Me How It's Done

Things Come So Natural
With The Ball In My Hand
Swishing Nets And Fancy Dribbles
This I Understand

Prejudice And Pain
Could Not Turn Me For A Loop
I Found Peace Of Mind
Whenever I Shot The Hoop

Acceptance Is Achieved
By The Talents You Possess
Keep Believing, Not Deceiving
And You Will Pass The Test

Life Is What You Make Of It
It Can Be A Very Hard Mission
But To Make The Road A Little Easier
Hold On To Your Religion.

I felt I was special at the age of five scoring the winning basket on my Uncle Everett's team. These games went on for many years. So when this sixth-grade boy challenged me at recess, I was more than ready to accept.

For the first time at Royce Elementary, I felt I had an edge over my fellow classmates.

When the one-on-one game started, I was doing fancy dribbles, trick shots and a lot of smack talking about how I was going to beat my opponent. All of a sudden, I looked up and noticed the crowd. Students of all ages, and even a few teachers, had gathered and were cheering for me as I was taking it to Mr. Sixth Grader. I was excited because people were enjoying watching me play basketball. Heck, I was entertaining the masses.

After that day on the basketball court, students of all ages and grades started treating me differently. I wasn't Tony the black kid anymore—I was Tony the basketball player. Students started seeing me as something other than a minority.

Things Always Happen on Time

As the school year went on, a few other black students enrolled at Royce. I was excited to see other students of color, but most did not stay very long. Some were suspended for fighting, and others left in discouragement when they found they just could not fit in at a white school. It made me sad when they left.

I felt really bad for one black student who ended up in a boys' home because of repeated delinquent activity. This made it clear to me at an early age how important our family's love, structure, and above all faith in God had been in creating my foundation. My family was very religious, and we felt all things were possible through our faith in the Almighty. My mother always used to tell me, "Things may not happen when you want them to, but through God they always happen on time."

My remaining years at Royce Elementary were great. I excelled academically and athletically. My sixth-grade basketball coach, Ms. Tucker, ran an offense called "Give It to Tony." Wherever I was on the court at that time, I'd get the ball and shoot. Ms. Tucker's coaching style is probably one of the reasons I became a high scorer through my many years of competitive basketball.

I would run home after a basketball game and yell, "Mom! Dad! Guess how many points I scored in the game?" My mom would say, "How many?" and I would yell something like, "27 points." But my parents would only say, "Oh yeah? That's nice." I wanted them to say more, but that's all I would get from them. I really don't think they believed I had scored that many points. Finally after about five games, my dad came to see me play. During our warmup, as I was pulling up a pair of knee-high, black knit socks, I looked up and was thrilled to see my father entering the gymnasium.

That game I put on a shooting exhibition, scoring 29 points and 15 rebounds. That game sparked my parents to start attending my sporting events from then on. My parents worked different hours, but one of them was always in attendance when their schedules allowed. That same year, my Royce Elementary basketball team came within one game of the city championship. The school that eliminated us was Burdge Elementary. My old buddies at Burdge beat us by one point, and from that time on I understood that Royce had become a part of me. Though I continued my neighborhood friendships, when it came to cheering for the winner, Royce was the one I chose. After my sixth-grade year, I was actually sad to leave Royce Elementary. I had established many friendships.

I sometimes wonder if the students and faculty at Royce Elementary ever really accepted my race at that time. Did they like me because of who I was as a person or only as a good basketball player? In the end, it really doesn't matter because the students, the faculty, and I left there better people. We all became more aware of cultures different from our own.

Chapter Two

Bluster

My mother's father, Arnett Henry Sr.—whom we all called by his nickname, "Bluster"—grew up in Mississippi in a very poor family. My grandmother would joke that when she was a child, she and her family would pass by the Henry place on their way to church on Sunday mornings, and they would see Bluster and his siblings running around their yard naked. The children would run and hide in the bushes until the horse and buggy passed by. It wasn't that they didn't know any better; they simply didn't have many clothes, and what outfits they did own were kept nice in a closet, not used at playtime when they could be soiled or torn.

My grandfather never denied the story. On the contrary, he himself often told stories about how poor he was growing up. Once he was reading a magazine story about the famous basketball player Wilt Chamberlain. The magazine featured pictures of Wilt's fabulous mansion, and it was reported that in Wilt's bedroom he could push a button and the ceiling would open up to the sky. Bluster was unimpressed. "Shoot," he commented, "when I was a little boy I could see the stars through my ceiling too, but we had holes in the roof; we didn't need a button to push."

Bluster was a religious man and often shared life stories that had a meaningful message. He often talked of life during the Jim Crow era, the time when all over the South, racist legislation known as "Jim Crow" laws kept blacks separate from whites. While these laws were in effect, from the late 1800s to the late 1960s, blacks were forbidden to use the same restaurants, bathrooms, and drinking fountains as whites. They had to occupy separate railroad cars and sit on seats at the back of the bus. They also faced restrictions in employment and voter rights, to name just a few.

Bluster grew up when things were separate but definitely not equal. He was blessed to have gotten a truck-driving job, making deliveries overnight and into the early hours of the morning in the early 1940s. Bluster said that often he would get hungry while driving and wanted to stop for something to eat, but he had to be very careful because stopping at the wrong locations could cost him his life. He would look for colored-owned restaurants or take a chance at a white establishment that might serve colored people in the rear of the restaurant. Bluster said "there was many a night" he just kept driving and went hungry because it was not safe to stop in certain towns or restaurants. He was always delighted when he found a colored-owned establishment.

Until the day he died in 1988, Bluster always spoke to white people with exaggerated politeness, addressing them as Mr. or Mrs. and saying "yes, sir" and "yes, ma'am," no matter what their age. This bothered me when I reached high school, and one day I built up enough confidence to challenge him on these mannerisms. I had always viewed Bluster as a very strong man, but I felt he displayed weakness when bowing down to white people.

"Bluster," I said, "Why do you address whites as sirs and ma'ams? Times have changed! It's the '70s now. You don't have to do that anymore." I then got cocky and said, "If I had grown up during your era, they would have had to kill me, because I never would have bowed down to nobody."

Bluster sat me down and explained a few things. He said that all his life, and especially during his time of driving trucks, he had to do or say whatever it took to get a paycheck. Even though in his heart he knew he was equal to them, he had been conditioned during his young years to take an inferior role to white people in order to survive in a world where whites held all the power. He took the dehumanizing treatment for one reason and one reason only—he had four little children who depended on him, and he loved his family enough to sacrifice anything for them—even his pride. "There is nothing greater than the love of Christ and the love you have for your family," he told me.

Bluster was the greatest grandfather I could ever have had. He was diagnosed with cancer in 1988 and given six months to live. When he told me about his diagnosis, he said, "Boy, I'm not scared to die, but what I will miss is that I won't get to see my family anymore." A month later, he died. We miss Bluster.

Chapter Three
Big Momma

My maternal grandmother's name was Opal (Ball) Henry, but she was always known as "Big Momma" to her family and friends. Big Momma was a loving, caring, jolly woman who would find humor in the many struggles of her past, but I know deep down inside they bothered her.

The second youngest of 10 children in Mississippi, Big Momma had lost both her mother and father by the age of 11, and was primarily raised by older siblings. Unfortunately, she did not have photographs or many memories of her parents to share with her children and grandchildren. Like many black people in the South, the Balls had white blood in their family. In fact, several of Big Momma's siblings had blue eyes and fair skin, and some of her cousins were 100 percent white. Big Momma recalled how the white and black cousins never acknowledged one another in public or even in private. I once asked her how hard was it for her and her siblings to know these were blood cousins and they could not talk to them because they were black. "There was love from both sides of the color line," Big Momma said, "and it was known and felt. But the way of the South at that time would not accept the family bond."

All her life, Big Momma worked hard. As a child, she'd had to do her share of chores on the farm. Her work ethic was "Work and work until it gets done." She had a presence and a touch that could heal a wounded heart, and a spirit to motivate the unmotivated. As an adult, Big Momma was known for being a great cook and housekeeper. She not only took care of her own children, but was also the "Mammy," or nanny, to the white children in the "big house" on the plantation where they lived.

All throughout the later years of her adult life, Big Momma spoke of a little girl named Betty Alice, one of the white children she cared for back on the plantation. She had a special bond with Betty Alice, whom she loved almost as one of her own children. One evening when Betty Alice's parents had gone out to dinner, Big Momma prepared a fancy meal as a treat for her and the little girl to share. She thought that since the two of them were alone, they could have some fun together. After the dinner was prepared, she made a plate for Betty Alice and set it on the table in the dining room. Then Big Momma made one mistake. She prepared a plate for herself and placed it at the table next to Betty Alice. The girl looked up at her with scorn in her eyes. "What are you doing?" she demanded. "Niggers don't eat at the big table, you need to go in the back and eat your dinner."

After she finished sharing that story, I said to Big Momma, "I know you let that little girl know what time it was, didn't you? What did you do, Big Momma? Tell me!"

And I remember the expression on Big Momma's face when she said that she took her plate and went to the back of the house to eat her dinner. Even after all these years, I can still see the pain and hurt in my grandmother's eyes, reflecting a sorrow that had stayed with her all this time. To this day, it pains me to think of my own grandmother being treated this way by a child she loved, and it sickens me to think of how this innocent child had been poisoned by racism and ignorance to believe she was superior to a black person.

I speak today for my grandparents, who, living in a profoundly racist society, were never given the right to speak up for themselves. My grandparents made me what I am today as well as what I become tomorrow. I thank my grandparents for teaching me to love and not to hate. Even though they encountered countless injustices during their lifetime, they never lowered themselves to hate whites or people of any other race. I thank my grandparents for teaching me to treat people the way that I want to be treated. I thank my grandparents for teaching me to love and respect everyone in the human race, and stressing that we are all in this world together.

Big Momma passed away in 1989 after a battle with Alzheimer's disease. Even prior to her death, with so much of her memory and communication fading away, she still would speak about little Betty Alice in a loving and mothering way.

Chapter Four
Mother

My mother, Farrie (Henry) Carr, was a mentor, a friend, a counselor, and spiritual leader—you name it, and that is what she was to me. She was a unique person in many ways, beginning with her name. I have never met another person in my life with the name of Farrie. Even though she never cared for the name, I think it suited her, because she was one of a kind. My mother was a very spiritual person with the ability to see what others could not. Over the years, she had visions and dreams of family members' unexpected deaths and misfortunes. My mother viewed the visions as a gift from God. She and I often spoke of these visions and dreams, although she did not tell many other people for fear of what they might think.

My mother grew up in the small town of Pontotoc, Mississippi. After she graduated high school, she attended Okolona Technical College and worked as a student teacher for young children. Then, in 1951, when she was 19, her family moved north to Beloit, Wisconsin, where my grandfather had a job opportunity in the booming steel industry at a company called Fairbanks and Morse. The Henrys were just one of countless black families to move north during the so-called Great Migration, a long-term movement of southern blacks to the urban north in search of better wages, better education, voting rights, legal rights, and better living conditions. The Great Migration went on from about 1916 to 1970.

The oldest of four children, my mother helped to raise her three younger siblings, Arnett Jr., Everett, and Jeanette, while my grandparents both worked. Growing up, she was often sick and frail. When I was a child, I can remember her often having migraine headaches so bad she could not lift up her head. But what my mother lacked in physical strength she made up for in mental strength and desire, for she was the great pretender. No matter how bad she felt, she could pull herself together to look well and complete a task.

I could talk to my mother about anything, and I truly felt more educated and energized after talking with her. Mother never dwelled on the racial problems she experienced growing up in the South, for she said her life was in God's hands and her walk was by faith and not by sight. When she did talk to us about the racism of her childhood, I know that she softened the stories in order to shield my brother and me from the real ugly situations she encountered. We have all heard the story of Rosa Parks, a brave woman who in 1955 refused to give up her seat on a bus to a white person. Her heroism led to the desegregation of buses in Montgomery, Alabama, and sparked the Civil Rights movement. The story of Rosa Parks really hit home for me when I talked to my mother, and she recalled sitting on the back of the bus as a teenager in Mississippi. At the time, Mother accepted it as the way things were. However, she did talk about how degrading it was to have to pull a curtain in the back of the bus, separating the blacks from the whites.

Mother's school experience in her formal learning years was a one-room schoolhouse in Pontotoc, Mississippi. There were 35 to 40 students of all different grades put together in one room. My mother really enjoyed the education and kinship at the colored-only school. She told us many positive stories and shared photos of her classmates. She was especially proud of her experience on the girls' basketball team—yes, she too was a basketball player!

I miss Mom. We lost her in August of 2002. At my mother's funeral, the Reverend read my mother's obituary, which described her as "Farrie Carr, graduate of Pontotoc School for the colored." I looked at my brother and said, "Wow, that's right—Mom went to a colored-only school!" As I viewed my mother for the last time, I flashed back to some of her stories she had told us about her early school experiences.

When my mother died, a part of me died also. Her spirit lives through me as I speak at many venues and share her legacy and life. I speak in her honor, and her presence is always felt. My mother loved her family more than life, and she instilled in my brother and me the idea that we could achieve anything that we dedicated our minds to. In her honor, my first daughter was named Francesca Farrie Carr. My mother passed away one week after Francesca's first birthday.

Chapter Five

Dad

My father, Robert Carr, was born in Jackson, Tennessee, the youngest of 10 children. His mother, Mary, had Native American blood, and long straight hair that hung past the middle of her back. She would always say "Indians don't die, they just fade away." My grandmother did exactly that, living to the age of 96 before passing away in 1985.

All her life, Grandma Carr cared for my dad's oldest brother, Chester, who was born mentally and physically challenged. Chester was very respectful, always greeting people as "Brother" or "Sister." Although he was mentally challenged, he amazed me as a youth by how well he could quote verses from the Bible. Growing up with Chester as an uncle really opened my eyes to people with disabilities at a very early age. I was so sad when Chester passed away in 1970.

My paternal grandfather's name was A. B. Carr. I have only seen one picture of him in my life, and he was tall and handsome. He died when my father was only nine years old. My dad's father was a butcher for wealthy white families in Jackson as well as a sharecropper and handyman. According to my father, Grandpa Carr was a jack-of-all-trades and a very hard-working man, and had a very strong physical presence.

The work ethic of my grandfather shined in my father also. Dad was an athlete and a very self-confident man. I always viewed my father as strong and never believed there was any weakness in him until one day when I was about ten years old. It was the early 1970s, and my family was traveling through the South. We had stopped at a gas station in a small town in Mississippi. Back in those days, every gas station had an attendant who pumped the gas for you. My brother and I sat in the car watching as the young attendant, who couldn't have been any older than 16, pumped the gas. When the kid was done, he told my dad the total and asked for the money. My dad paid him and was waiting for his change.

What happened next shocked as well as educated me as to what my parents had to go through growing up in the South. When the young employee brought back my father's change, he said haughtily, "Here you go—and call me sir."

My brother and I, having grown up in the North, were not about to take this insult. We cried out indignantly, "I know he did not say to call him sir!" and begged our dad to let us set the boy straight. But my father, visibly upset, warned us not to say another word. He then looked in the young employee's face and said "Thank you, sir." The young employee demanded, "What did you say?" And my father had to respond by saying "Thank you, sir," once again.

As we pulled out of the gas station parking lot, my brother and I were enraged and mortified. We immediately questioned our father as to why he called that young punk "Sir," especially after the kid had used such a disrespectful tone of voice. My father calmly said, "Because I want our family to live to see another day." After that, my brother and I didn't say much because for the next 50 miles, we observed our father fearfully watching his rearview mirror. For the first time, we understood that there was real danger in the South for black people who stood up for themselves. My father had allowed himself to be shamed in order to protect us.

My father did not like to talk about his experiences during the Jim Crow era, but two years prior to his death he did share a story that I'll never forget. My father always bragged about how many girlfriends he had as a youth. One night, he said, he was on a date with a young lady he really wanted to impress, and he took her to downtown Jackson to see a movie. At that time in Tennessee, the blacks in the community had a curfew, but my father and his date were having so much fun that they lost track of time. As he and his date were exiting the movie theater, they were approached by a police officer.

"Boy, do you know what time it is?" the officer asked. Before my father could answer, he was struck in the head with the officer's nightstick. Now, I had noticed growing up that my father had a scar on his forehead, but I had always assumed he received it while playing sports. After he shared this story, I realized he had been carrying this scar from that dreadful incident for most of his life. What a terrible reminder it must have been for him to look at that scar on a daily basis. Knowing my father, he blocked out that difficult time in his life and just closed that chapter, while only giving me a glimpse of the painful moments of his past.

My father passed away in May of 2004. As we laid my father to rest and I viewed his body for the very last time, guess what I saw and will always remember—the scar! I wish my father would have shared more stories about growing up in the South as a child, but I know he didn't want to look back at a time that was very hard and difficult for him. He shielded his children from the cruelty and inequities that he endured in his life, and focused on the fun and positive times he and his family experienced.

Chapter Six

Changes

All of my family's past experiences helped to develop the person that I became and continue to evolve into as I grow older. My junior high school (seventh and eighth grade) experiences were great. At Lincoln Junior High, I reunited with many of my friends from the old neighborhood once again.

There was one dramatic change that took place during that time. My parents had decided that the old neighborhood was becoming very unsafe and they wanted to move into a safer environment. Then one night, in September of 1971, an intruder tried to open the back door of our home. My father was not home, as he worked nights, so my mother got her .38 revolver and told my brother and me to stand behind her as she approached the door. The intruder must have heard the chamber revolve as my mom cocked the gun and held it up against the door, because he quickly disappeared. We went back to bed, but I'm sure mom kept the gun close at hand the rest of the evening.

After this incident, we moved to the west side of town into an all-white neighborhood, although my father recalled that all the time they were searching for a house, the realtor tried to steer them into African American neighborhoods. At that time, whites feared that once a black family moved into the neighborhood, the value of their homes would drop. This move was a dream and a hope for my parents for a very long time, and I was happy and supportive of my parents achieving this dream. However, moving from a predominantly African American neighborhood to an all-exclusive white neighborhood had its challenges. I remember the morning we moved into our new home. Every white family in the neighborhood, it seemed, had pulled up chairs or gathered on the sidewalk to watch. The expressions of dismay on their faces said it all: "There goes the neighborhood!"

The neighbors' attitude disgusted me. Inside, I thought, "We have just as much of a right to live in this neighborhood as you." As for my parents, they appeared unaware of the hostility, as they kept on moving furniture as if nothing were going on. It was as if they blocked out everything around them and just stayed on task to complete the move.

I decided to ignore the neighbors, too. Spotting a very nice basketball hoop above the garage of our new home, I grabbed my basketball and shot the ball at the basket, and swish! Right through the net. I said to myself, "Yeah, this is going to be all right." I proceeded into the garage, where I spotted some toys and garbage that the previous residents had failed to throw away. As I sifted through the pile I was delighted to find a book about the Osmond Brothers, a famous white family musical group that was all the rage at the time. I continued to explore, and I found a cereal box with a cut-out record on it from the Jackson 5, an all-black group featuring lead singer Michael Jackson. I was thrilled to find the record until I noticed that someone had scratched off the words Jackson 5 and written Nigger 5 in its place. Reading the hateful words Nigger 5 bothered me even more than the rude stares of the neighbors. I destroyed the record before anyone in my family could see it and never mentioned to my parents what I had found, for I did not want them to be saddened during this very special time in their lives.

Within thirty to ninety days, many of the residents in our new neighborhood put their houses up for sale and began to depart. This was a confusing time in my life, a time when I had many questions and needed answers. During this time, I found a mentor in my favorite teacher ever my seventh grade social studies instructor, Mr. Lowery. He demanded respect and discipline in his classroom, and he shared a quote that lives with me to this day. The quote was "Not only to accept, but to ask the question 'why?'" Every test or quiz we had in Mr. Lowery's class contained this quote and was to be recited in its exact format. This quote resonated with me at a time when I was starting to question the world around me—to ask why things were the way they were. I just could not accept some of the injustices that I saw in the world around me.

This was also a period in time where I really started understanding the love that my grandparents had for me. I had always loved my grandparents, but now that I was struggling to adjust to my new home environment, they became more important to me than ever. Some of the best times in my life were spent sitting at my grandparents' kitchen table listening to them quote Bible scriptures and apply those scriptures to everyday life. It was there at that kitchen table where they began educating me about my heritage. These sessions with my grandparents taught me to walk tall and to be proud of what and who I am.

My grandparents gave me a wealth of education that could never be matched by any educational institution. I found myself starving to learn more from them about my family history, and every session seemed more interesting. These sessions went on from seventh grade until I finished college in 1983. I would drive four hours every weekend before and after the basketball season to get my education from the two of them. It became a way of life for me. Their lessons and advice helped me to open up and accept many new friends in my new neighborhood.

With my father working nights and my mother working days, I began to establish new friendships through athletics, and soon my neighborhood was becoming a community of trust. My mother became involved in car-pooling with other parents, transporting kids to school and athletic activities. After a year's time, my new house finally became a home. I still credit my grandparents for teaching me self-confidence and respect for all. After all my grandparents had been through growing up in Mississippi, they taught me to turn the other cheek. In many instances it was the only way to succeed until the opportunity afforded me a time to really speak my mind on controversial issues related to race.

The new neighborhood was home, but I still remained in contact and missed my friends from the old 'hood. Some of those old friends called my family sellouts or Uncle Toms for moving out of the black community, but those who were true friends still came to visit. Fortunately we all attended the same junior high school, so I could see them daily, unlike when I was in fourth, fifth, and sixth grade at Royce Elementary.

Chapter Seven
Student Athlete

I became a very popular student athlete while attending Lincoln Junior High School, where I was reunited with old friends and created many new friendships with students from all over the west side of Beloit. I was fortunate to excel in basketball, and my eighth-grade team won the overall championship. While at Lincoln I started to have some interest in girls, but basketball remained my one true love.

Junior high was fun, and the time seemed to fly by far too quickly. After finishing seventh and eighth grade, it was time for high school. I was excited because I had the opportunity to go to school on the east side of Beloit, where the majority of students were black. My ninth and tenth grade years were at a school called Aldrich. At the start of my freshman year, I began training for basketball. At that time I was only about five foot seven and very skinny, and a sophomore took one look and said I'd never make the varsity team because I was too small. That boy really motivated me to work hard and try to become the best player I could be. I finished that year as the leading scorer and our team was number one in the conference. When I returned to school as a sophomore, I had grown five inches and added about 10 pounds. Everyone was shocked to see the physical change in me. About halfway through the basketball season, I was moved up to the varsity team. Ironically, the person I replaced on the team was the very same boy who had said I would never make varsity.

Aldrich was an enriching experience, but I looked forward to going to the big high school, Beloit Memorial High on the west side of town, where I would spend my eleventh and twelfth-grade years. As a child, I could look out the window of our house and see the high school I was always excited watching the older students who passed by our house on the way to school.

Beloit Memorial was a dream come true for me. I could not have had a better experience. I became a first team All-Conference and All-State Basketball player, and voted Most Valuable player of my team my junior and senior year, and I thrived academically, too, achieving high honor roll status all of my senior year. Our varsity basketball team was always ranked in the top five in the state of Wisconsin. I had a diverse group of friends that included students of all races, rich and poor, and mentally and physically challenged. I was voted both prom and homecoming king while attending high school. The time again flew by much too quickly, and my grandparents continued to keep me grounded and humbled while reminding me that all things are possible through God Almighty.

During my senior year in high school, I was told that many colleges and universities were scouting me for athletic scholarships. One Big Ten school scouted me aggressively and the college staff got to know my family very well. During my senior year in 1978, my team lost the state championship to Neenah, Wisconsin after we gave up a 17-point lead in the third quarter. I fouled out of the championship game, which was odd because I had never fouled out of a game before at any level of playing basketball. It took a very long time to get over that loss.

That spring, after basketball season was over, it was time to make a decision about college. My basketball coach had a policy that active players could not receive any letters of acceptance or correspondence for he felt it would be a distraction to players and the team. Players received all letters at the end of their senior year. Until then, all inquires and letters had to go through him. Finally, one day that spring, Coach handed over our college letters. That day was both happy and sad. I was shocked when I saw that my teammate Bob Grady had received a large box of college letters, and all mine could fit into a shoebox. There was not even a letter of acceptance from the Big Ten college that had been courting me all year. When I asked Coach about the Big Ten school, he responded that he had never gotten any letter from them and that everything that came was in the box. I felt shaken and uneasy. Something did not feel right

Suddenly, Coach began speaking highly about a state school, the University of Wisconsin-Eau Claire, and encouraged me to attend. I was familiar with Eau Claire because Coach would take Beloit players to a basketball camp there every summer. Beloit players had dominated at the Eau Claire basketball camp in the summer of 1977, my junior year of high school. The coach at Eau Claire was nationally recognized, but I had no desire to go to school there, in large part because in the late 1970s and 1980s, Eau Claire was a white community with very few minorities. Of the university's student body of some 11,000, only a handful were African or African American.

The month of June was rapidly approaching and I had not decided where I would be attending college. My friends had already chosen their colleges shortly after the last senior basketball game. Bob Grady received a scholarship to Northwestern University and my friend Perry Range from South Beloit, Illinois chose the University of Illinois. I knew I was just as good as they were, and many basketball observers said my skill level was higher than that of my friends. Everyone in our community had assumed that I would be attending a Big Ten or major college basketball program, and so had I. But now, no schools were calling me, except for smaller state schools or junior colleges, and I started getting nervous.

I called the Big Ten university that I had been expecting to offer me a scholarship. Representatives from the university had attended all my high school games, and they had befriended my family, so I naturally had expected the school to make me an offer. I reached the assistant coach, and he sadly reported that he had resigned his position and that the head coach had decided to offer their last scholarship to a kid from Chicago instead of me. I was crushed.

The next day, I verbally committed to the University of Wisconsin-Eau Claire, a school that did not offer athletic scholarships. The Eau Claire community was excited about signing a player of my caliber, but I was less than enthusiastic; I just felt I should have been somewhere else. When I shared my reservations with my grandfather, however, he put my decision in perspective. He reminded me that I was going to college first and foremost to get an education, and basketball was secondary to my purpose. "You are good enough to play anywhere and against anyone," he added. "And if you hope to play beyond college, it doesn't matter where you go to school." After our discussion, I was confident that Eau Claire was the right choice for me.

The decision was made and negative press releases were to follow. Some fans and reporters from Beloit felt I was selling myself short by attending a small university instead of a major college. Even my friends from the old neighborhood questioned why I wanted to go to Eau Claire. I was 17 years old at the time and I felt that not only did I let myself down, but my community as well. But I had made up my mind to attend the university at Eau Claire, and I would remain true to my decision.

That same month, June of 1978, while I was coming to terms with my college decision, I received some thrilling news. I had been chosen by the U.S. Olympic Sports Festival Committee to compete in the Olympic trials in Colorado Springs. I felt it was a great honor because the committee had chosen only 48 candidates nationwide to attend the trials. In the second week of July, I packed my bags and boarded a airplane en route to the Olympic Training Center.

The training center was an exciting place. I saw and met many players and coaches that I had read about in Street and Smiths, a popular sporting news magazine. Many of the players had been basketball stars since the eighth grade and knew each other from national basketball camps they had attended as youths. No one knew me. The first question was "Where are you from?" and the second question was "Where are you going to college?" Both questions made me uncomfortable because no one knew where Beloit, Wisconsin was, and mentioning Eau Claire only brought on more looks of confusion. I was always confident and a little cocky, so I responded by saying, "Well, you may not have heard of Beloit or Eau Claire now, but by the end of the trials when you witness my game you won't ever forget the names of those cities."

I celebrated my golden eighteenth birthday while attending the trials in Colorado Springs. It was a great gift to be playing the game I had loved since the age of 5, and with the best players in the nation. In the last four days of the Olympic trials, we divided into teams by region, and I was chosen as a starter for the Midwest Team. My parents and my mother's sister, Aunt Jeanette, ventured to Colorado Springs from Beloit to see the games live. I was so proud to represent the Midwest and to have my family share in the experience. On the last day of the trials, there was an Olympic parade for all the athletes from all the Olympic sports. The 48 basketball players from all over the United States became a fraternity. We all said our goodbyes on the night of the parade, knowing that this was an event we would never forget.

As I returned to Beloit, my attitude and basketball skills were better than ever. My friends often commented on how much I changed as a person since going to Colorado Springs. Now that I had played with the best players from all over the U.S., people wanted to know if I was still planning to go to UW Eau Claire, a school that did not have the big name of colleges like North Carolina, UCLA, Notre Dame, and Louisville. Many of the players I had met at the Olympic trials were attending those big-name schools, and they all told me I was good enough to play there, too—so why was I going to attend Eau Claire? I really did not have an answer for them, but only said that I would play hard no matter where I ended up.

Chapter Eight
Higher Education

The month of August came, and I packed my bags for Eau Claire. My mother and father drove me to the university. It was a sad drive for both my parents and me because we both knew I would never live with them again. During the four-hour drive through the heart of Wisconsin, my father gazed out at the roadside farms and lumberyards and talked about his duties as a sharecropper and woodchopper. His stories really made the ride seem shorter. My mother, though, was very quiet during the whole trip for she knew this was a goodbye for her baby boy. Mother was always a very emotional person when it came to goodbyes.

As we arrived on campus and found my dormitory, Horan Hall, which housed many other student athletes, we found that many of the students were anticipating my arrival. I heard them shouting, "He's here—Carr is here!" The basketball community was very happy to see me in person. After we moved all my belongings into the dorm, it was time to say that dreadful and sad goodbye. My father shook my hand. There were tears in his eyes as he whispered, "Take care of business." My mother cried, and reminded me to put God first in everything. I felt so sad that I didn't know how to respond. As they left, I watched them from my dorm window until they were out of sight. Then I finally started to cry, and I could not hold back my tears. I wished I were in the car with them heading back to Beloit, but I knew I had a commitment and a responsibility to live up to. I kept thinking about all the things my grandfather had conditioned in my heart and soul, which was my way of coping with all the challenges to come.

The hardest adjustment was getting used to dorm life. I hated Sundays because everyone in the dorms was watching the Green Bay Packers. My roommate, also on the basketball team, had grown up near Green Bay, as had many of his friends, and they would gather in our dorm to watch the games. The first football Sunday in Eau Claire I decided to go outside and shoot some baskets. As I came back into the dorm and was approaching my room, I heard the shout "Run, nigger, run!" The students were cheering on an African American Packer player who was running for a touchdown on the television screen.

I turned right around and walked away in disgust. Looking for someone to vent with, I went to see my friend John Washington, a fellow African American on the basketball team who also lived in Horan Hall. Like me, John had been born in Beloit, but went to high school in Racine, Wisconsin. I found John in his room. "You won't believe what I just heard, man!" I told him. "I heard these guys on my floor yelling 'Nigger!' at the television screen."

"Yeah, I know, get used to it," John said grimly. "It happens a lot in this dorm."

John was a year older than me and had lived in the dorm the previous year. I felt sorry for him because he'd had to put up with racial negativity a whole year all by himself, as the only African American in Horan Hall. By now, it was as though he had given up on educating people about race. I suppressed my feelings, too, for the time being—resolving to say something about the racist remarks the next time I heard them. For now, John and I went back outside to channel our negative energies through a game of one-on-one.

On October 15, 1978, the basketball season started. I was happy to get going because basketball was my way of dealing with stress and frustration. Although he never told me so until the season started, Eau Claire's coach had actually recruited me to be a point guard, an offensive position that involved very little shooting but focused on ball handling and passing. The previous year, the team had lost to the University of Wisconsin–Parkside and missed going to the national tournament because they lacked a good ball handler on point. I was to be the new ball handler to get Eau Claire past UW Parkside.

When practice started, I realized I was much quicker and more athletic than many of my teammates. The first thirteen games into the season were nothing but fun. John Washington and I were the two starting guards, and we dominated all the teams we went up against. In the fourteenth game, however, John was abruptly removed from the starting lineup and received very little playing time from then on. He was replaced by another team member who had been suspended for the first thirteen games. The change in the lineup upset me, for I felt that John had earned his starting position. Besides, John was not only a friend, but we had a created a great chemistry on the court, and his being gone affected my game. John and I at that time were the only two African Americans on the team. In fact, during my whole four-year career at UW Eau Claire, there were never more than three African Americans on the team at one time.

UW Eau Claire's coach at that time wanted me to shoot less and pass more. I was committed to doing what he asked because I wanted to do what was best for the team. That year, we made it to the district finals to once again face UW Parkside, the team that had eliminated Eau Claire the previous year. Playing the game the way the coach wanted, I handled the ball against intense pressure and gave up shots that I could have easily made in favor of passing to my teammates. I finished the game with only 3 points, but the important thing was that we won the game, 61-58. Coach's plan had worked in defeating Parkside. I was happy, but felt I could do so much more for the team if the coach would allow me to shoot more.

One week later, we were on our way to the National Association of Intercollegiate Athletics in Kansas City, Missouri. I was excited because I knew we would meet the best of the best in this small-college national tournament. I was also very excited because my parents and Aunt Jeanette would be traveling to Kansas City to watch me play. I decided I would become more aggressive in the tournament than I had in previous games, because we were now in the national spotlight, and the teams we were up against were more athletic and skilled. I started shooting and scoring whenever I could, racking up the points at will. Coach wanted to win so he didn't try to stop me. Meanwhile, some of my teammates had problems creating shots and competing against players who were much quicker and athletic at a national level. That worked great for me because I was a true scorer and could get my shot off against opposing defenses.

We lost in the third round of the tournament, but I caught the eye of many observers, most importantly a National Basketball Association scout named Marty Blake. After that first basketball season in Eau Claire, I immediately started receiving calls from college basketball recruiters and coaches who had read about my performance in the national tournament and wondered what had happened to me over for the past year. A number of these coaches remembered me from my senior year in high school.

A theme started developing when time and again, coaches and recruiters reported they had tried to contact me during my senior year in Beloit, only to be told by my high school coach that I was committed to another university. Many of the recruiters interested in me were from major universities with great academic and basketball programs. Some offered to transfer me with a full scholarship, but there was one catch: as a transfer, I would have to sit out of basketball for one year. One year without competitive basketball was not an option for me. I loved the game way too much to sit out. After careful consideration, I decided to stay at Eau Claire.

Naturally, I was still very upset by the knowledge that major college coaches had not been able to contact me my senior year in high school. I hated to think of what that might mean. But in the end, I decided to block it all out and focus on my life at the time. When the freshman year ended, I began preparing for my return to the Colorado Springs Olympic Training Center.

Chapter Nine

Challenges

That summer of 1979, I was invited back to the Olympic trials in preparation for the World University games. While training in Colorado Springs, I met a player named Andrew Toney, a stellar player who would later go on to win a NBA championship with the Philadelphia 76ers. Andrew taught me a lot and probably never realized it. For the first time in years, I was playing against a person whom I considered a better basketball player than myself. He was very smart and strong. Although he was not gifted with great jumping ability, he more than made up for it in determination and strength. Andrew frustrated me because my tricks of the trade did not work against him. He challenged me and forced me to improve my game.

One day during practice, I injured my back and had to leave the training camp. The whole time I was in physical therapy, I followed Andrew's example and kept a positive attitude, focusing on gaining more muscle and strength to add to my game. Upon my return from Colorado, I headed back to UW Eau Claire for the start of my sophomore year. I was looking forward to a great season. With a year under my belt, I felt I was ready for anything that might come my way.

In the end, I was very glad I stayed in Eau Claire after the many tempting offers that had come my way after the national tournament, because my sophomore year was great. I became a scoring machine and our team was once again a national contender. My parents came to Eau Claire more frequently to watch the team play, and the UW Eau Claire staff and the community made my parents feel very welcome at the games.

There was something else that made my sophomore year special: I had a girlfriend that I really cared about. Lisa had been one of my classmates from Royce Elementary years before, and as fate would have it, a mutual friend re-introduced us while I was on a weekend visit to Beloit and we began dating. She continued to live in Beloit during my sophomore year, so we maintained a long-distance relationship. I could talk to Lisa about anything and everything—which added up to some very high monthly phone bills! My relationship with Lisa made my sophomore year go fast, for we had agreed the following year she would be attending the University of Eau Claire with me.

That year our team finished third in the nation, and I was featured in the national sporting news magazine Street and Smiths as a player to watch. I was proud because that was the magazine I always read in high school, and for me to have my picture in there was quite an honor.

Everything was going great until my junior year at UW Eau Claire. At first, things were looking up. I had been nationally recognized in many publications and looked forward to another basketball season. Lisa was at the university with me now. She would attend all of our home basketball games, and I looked forward to having someone from my hometown present at every game. Although Lisa was a very fair-skinned Caucasian, I never felt nervous about being involved in an interracial relationship in a white community. In fact, I rarely thought about the racial difference at all. Lisa's personality was what attracted me to her; it had nothing to do with the color of her skin. I loved Lisa because she was supportive and caring, but at the same time very independent. My family loved her too and accepted her without question. My grandfather, however, had fears and doubts. Being up north in Wisconsin, a relatively conservative area, I think he feared for my safety around people who had prejudice and bias.

When the basketball season began my junior year, it had a very strange feel to it. I noticed that the coach would frequently take me out of the game if I had a good scoring streak going. The only time he would let me play the whole game was when the score was close and he needed me to score. I felt that he had a grudge against me and this was his way of getting back at me. One weekend we went out of town for back-to-back games with another school. We had lost the Friday night game and Coach was very upset. The following day he called a team meeting in our hotel, and for some reason he chose to make an example out of me. In the middle of the meeting, Coach turned to me and said, "Hey Carr, do you like your teammates?" I said, "Yes, I like my team." Coach then said, "Well guess what? Your team don't like you." He then pointed to two of my teammates and said, "Hey, you don't like Carr, do you? Do you?" Put on the spot, the teammates had no choice but to tell the coach they didn't like me.

Coach then looked at me and said, "You don't like your teammates, Carr, but you like white women, don't you?" I was shocked and embarrassed that he would make such a stupid racial statement to make a point. Before I could respond, he ended the conversation by warning me that I might lose my starting position for the next game. I was speechless.

To this day, I still do not know why the coach would make such a personal and degrading comment. I was so upset that I called my mother and father right after the team meeting and told them what he had said. They were just as angry as I was, but told me to ignore the coach because his racial comments had nothing to do with basketball. Then I thought about my options. This was my junior year of college, and I had established myself as an all-conference and all-american player. I considered that I could possibly transfer to another state school just so I could play against Eau Claire.

I did start the following game, but I played without much enthusiasm, and we lost a close game that we should have won. When I returned to Eau Claire after the road trip, I inquired about a potential transfer to another state college, but I knew that if I did pursue the transfer, it could create negative publicity both for myself and the team. In the end I decided to weather the storm and once again focus my energies on school, basketball and Lisa. I never informed Lisa of Coach's comment; I buried it deep inside my mind.

I finished my junior year with many honors, even though I felt I had a down year and could have done much better. The team finished in the final four in the nation, and I once again was blessed to be featured in Street and Smiths for a third consecutive year as the magazine's pick for Basketball All-American. The challenging year was over, and I made a promise to myself to go all out my senior year.

Chapter Ten

Top Cat

My senior year was a lot like my sophomore year—fun! We had a good team and it would be my farewell to Eau Claire after four years. I did not have any more conflict with the coach that year. He allowed to me to play the game with no limitations, as he recognized that my skills were leading us to bigger wins. As a result, I was very fortunate and blessed to establish many school records, which I still hold today. I am still the all-time leading scorer for the university, a record that has held for 29 years.

The games my senior year were very exciting and the fans were superb. All throughout senior year, crowds would cheer for me by the name TC, or Top Cat, a nickname that had been bestowed by our local radio play-by-play announcer. By the end of the season, I was known as Top Cat to all the students on campus. My mother in particular enjoyed the name because her favorite cartoon character was named Top Cat.

The community of Eau Claire was very accepting of me, even though the minority population was nonexistent. Sometimes in the local bar areas some drunk made an occasional racial comment, but I chalked it up to ignorance. At the same time, I was very careful to avoid bringing negative attention on myself by fighting or getting into verbal confrontations.

With a successful senior year of basketball behind me, I started concentrating on my skills in hopes of being drafted into the NBA. That June, I was invited to the 30th Anniversary Portsmouth Virginia Invitational Tournament 1982, which featured some of the best senior All-Stars in the nation. I was chosen as a starter for my team, and was thrilled to once again play with the best of the best. When the draft finally came around, I was very nervous. I knew that coming out of a small college like Eau Claire might be a disadvantage for me, as the NBA teams preferred players from Big Ten schools. Still, I felt there was a good chance the Washington Bullets would draft me as early as the second round. As it turned out, I was drafted by the Milwaukee Bucks in the sixth round, as their second-choice guard behind their number 1 pick Paul Pressey. Although I had expected to go earlier, I was happy to have an opportunity to compete, knowing that many players from big-time schools were drafted behind me. My two hometown friends Bob and Perry who had attended Big Ten schools were drafted after me in the seventh round. In the end, I realized, it really does not matter where you go to school; what matters is doing your best with the hand you are dealt.

I felt achievement being drafted to the National Basketball Association after playing in Beloit and completing four years at the University of Eau Claire. After I was drafted, however, Lisa and I began to drift apart. I blamed myself; I had put my concentration on basketball and unintentionally made her secondary. Lisa and I stayed in touch but our relationship would never be the same.

The NBA experience was not what I had hoped it would be. For one thing, while at camp I was shocked by the culture of the NBA and some of the immoral behavior of some players I met. I realized that many of the players that played the game I loved were not worthy of being seen as role models. The social life of the early eighties was a very interesting era in sports as well as in life. I also had trouble with meeting the expectations of the Milwaukee Bucks' coach, Don Nelson. I was in camp scoring baskets and playing very well, but that was not what Coach Nelson wanted. He wanted a point guard who could distribute the ball, leaving the scoring up to seasoned veterans to handle that part of the offense. However, I was too immature to realize that at this level I needed to follow the program of the coach and distribute the ball, for I was not the only scorer on this team.

While attending the Bucks tryouts, I felt discouraged and unhappy. Alone at night in the hotel, I began to question myself as to whether this was something I really wanted. Was this my destiny? At last I decided maybe I was just a bad fit for the team and another team would be better. My agent informed me that one of the Washington Bullets' top-drafted guards had been dismissed, and I saw this as an opportunity to leave Milwaukee and try out for the Bullets. However, the move turned out to be a mistake. I did not realize that my player rights were owned by the Bucks and it was not possible for me to try and join the Bullets. I should have had a better agent and been more informed.

At that point, I left professional basketball and decided to never play again. This was a decision that I regret to this day. I second-guessed myself and did not act on the principles that had gotten me this far, or maybe basketball was not my true purpose in life. For the next six years after leaving basketball, I found myself in a funk. When I left the Milwaukee Bucks I went back to Eau Claire for one more semester.

Above: My brother Steve and me in a milk advertisement ad in Beloit Wisconsin 1962.

Below: My Grade 5 class picture at Royce Elementary School. Can you find me?

Below: Grandfathers Chauffeur's License from 1947.
Note the "C" for colored classification under the race section.

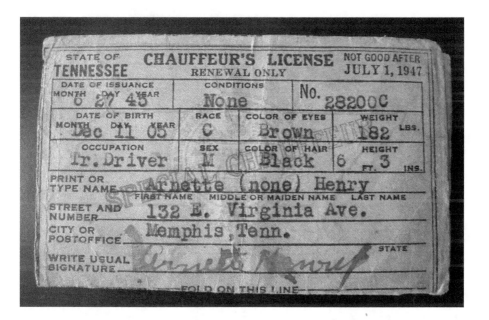

Above: Grandparents Arnett and Opal Henry.
Two of the most influential people in my life.

Below: J.R. Watkins Co. meeting in Memphis Tennessee 1941. Grandmother Mary Carr is in the 1st row 4th person from the left. Grandfather AB Carr is in the 5th row 2nd person from the left. This was one of his last photos. He past away 3 months after this meeting in Memphis.

Above: Mother Farrie Carr posing for the camera.

Right: Mother always talked about her basketball team. Here is a photo from the 1949-50 Pontotoc Colored High School basketball team. Mother is in the back row first from the left.

Above: Mother's High School Graduation photo from 1950.

Below: Mother's Diploma from Pontotoc Colored High School dated April 24, 1950.

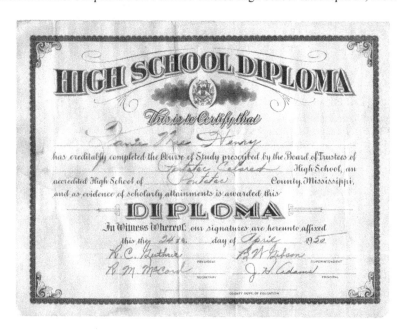

Above: My father posing for a photo at the age of 18.

Below: W.B. Kennedy Lodge photo from the late 1950's. Father is pictured in the back row 6th person from the left.

Jim Crow Era segregation sign from a railroad station. This is from my personal collection.

Nigger Head Stove Polish Tin from my personal collection.

NiggerHair Tobacco Pouch from my personal collection.

The 1982 National Association of Intercollegiate Athletics Basketball Championships in Kansas City Missouri. In this photo I was on my way to a 41-point performance, and another victory for the University of Wisconsin-Eau Claire Blugolds team.

My 4 Girls

Francesca Farrie Carr

Gionna Marie Carr

Eden Loretta Carr

Carmen Lee Carr

Chapter Eleven

Career

It was hard being in Eau Claire and not playing basketball. I could not even watch a game because it was too painful for me not to participate in the game I loved. Meanwhile, Lisa and I remained in a strained relationship, but started to communicate less and less over time. After I completed my final semester in Eau Claire, I moved to the Twin Cities and became the assistant basketball coach at Macalester College. Shortly after Lisa graduated in 1984, she moved and reunited with me in the Twin Cities of Minneapolis and St. Paul, Minnesota where we began our professional careers. I had fallen in love with the Twin Cities during my college years, when I would often travel there for shopping and to just get away.

Lisa and I grew apart even more in the Twin Cities, mostly because I was having trouble coping after giving up competitive basketball, and coaching was not filling the void. Whenever I watched professional games, I was reminded of the friends I had met in Colorado Springs who were now playing at the professional level, and I kicked myself because I could have been there, too. I was also depressed to discover that once I had stopped playing basketball, a lot of the people who I thought were my friends were no longer interested in hanging out with me. As the glory and fame from basketball disappeared, so had these so-called friends. It made me very bitter.

In January of 1986, after one year of coaching at Macalester, I was blessed to be hired by a company called Merrick, a vocational training site for mentally and physically challenged adults. I'd had the opportunity during college to run my own basketball camps, and I really enjoyed the love and appreciation I received from individuals with disabilities. I can remember even in high school I had a dear friend named Mike who was hearing impaired and could not speak. After basketball games, Mike and I would sit and communicate with pad and pen for hours. I know Mike really appreciated me taking the time to communicate with him, and I appreciated his friendship. These earlier experiences had taught me that working with people with disabilities might be a good career for me, and so I was enthusiastic about my job with Merrick.

When I started at Merrick, there were about 75 employees and I was the only employee of color. This was my first experience with cultural differences in a professional work environment. I felt I had to work much harder than my co-workers to achieve respect. Sometimes it was very draining because some of the management had preconceived ideas about me being a black man and an "ex-jock." Some had the stereotype that I was a dumb jock who would not be successful in this field. I did not give up, however; I just kept my competitive edge and focused on my job: helping the mentally challenged individuals that were in need. I got a lot of satisfaction in helping them develop job skills so that they could work and earn income. They were so appreciative, too, of the help we provided. Their love was unconditional, not related to basketball.

One day I was feeling especially frustrated at work, convinced I would never get the recognition I felt I had earned. I needed just a glimmer of hope, something that would give me the strength to get through another day. I was sitting at my desk completing paperwork when I heard the strains of an old African American spiritual coming from somewhere in the building. I followed the beautiful songs and there is where I found Hazel, a tiny, mentally challenged African American woman from Earlsborough, Oklahoma. The songs she was singing had special meaning to me because they were songs sung by my ancestors while they worked as slaves and later as sharecroppers in the fields of the South. They were songs of hope and inspiration that there would be better days ahead. I discovered that Hazel knew hundreds of songs, and she became my motivation to get through any day. If it were not for Hazel, my struggle at Merrick would have been much more difficult.

Over time, I advanced in my career at Merrick and spent 18 years with the company. I became a company director and, with the encouragement of executive director Kevin Martineau, I even developed a Diversity Committee with two co-directors at Merrick that helped change the company culture to a more open and tolerant one. I still thank Kevin, for he afforded me an opportunity to prove myself on a professional level. Kevin left Merrick in the late 1990s. The new executive director gave me yet another opportunity. I would become one of the company's representatives with a well-established local business organization.

I was very excited because this was a reputable organization that had done great things on a local and national level and was very well recognized and respected. Before I attended my first official meeting, I was warned that at the beginning of every gathering and before the business began, participants would sing an opening song. I said, "No problem, I can handle that." When I attended the meeting, the first thing I noticed was that I was the only person of color in the room. In fact, I figured I was probably the only person of color who had ever attended one of the local chapter's meetings. This made me feel like a bit of an outsider, a feeling that was amplified by the fact that people were not very quick to introduce themselves or welcome me to the meeting. Luckily, there was one person in attendance I knew.

When the meeting started, the president of the organization announced that it was time to sing the opening song. To my great discomfort, the song they had chosen was an African American spiritual, "Swing Low, Sweet Chariot." Although I thought that a slave song was an odd choice, I decided to give them the benefit of the doubt. It was a popular song, and perhaps they had only chosen it because it was well liked. As hard as it was, I tried to assimilate and sing the song along with my new fellow members. But to my horror, when the song was over, I heard a man shout, "Yessa, Massah!"

I said loudly, "I know I did not hear what I just heard," and at that point the same man—a well-respected local businessperson—yelled "Yessa, Massah!" once again. Apparently he thought it was a great joke to make fun of slaves. I waited, and no one else challenged the man's racist remark. That was when I decided I would no longer associate with this organization unless something was said about the inappropriate comments. No mention was ever made, and I later learned that the person who had made the comment was a past president of the organization's local chapter. Merrick remained a member of the organization, but from then on, I refused to be involved with them.

As I mulled over the experience, an old expression of my father's echoed in my mind: "The more things change, the more they stay the same." I decided not to take the incident personally, and turned the anger I had felt that day into determination. Now I was more motivated than ever to educate people and raise awareness about racial diversity.

Chapter Twelve

Love

As I look back on my relationship with my first love, Lisa, I realize that she and I had to go our separate ways to let each other grow. Lisa will always be special to me, for we shared in each other's development during the good and bad times growing from kids to adults, but once we set out on our own, we were no longer compatible. Sometime after I first started my career at Merrick in 1986, Lisa and I officially ended our relationship after seven years together.

After the breakup, I was fortunate to date many wonderful women of many different cultures. The people I met and dated from other cultures really helped mold me and educate me about diversity. It's ironic that over my lifetime I only had three very serious relationships. Coincidentally, all three of these ladies were born in the month of December and each had at least two sisters and no brothers.

One weekend when I was visiting my mother in Beloit, she pulled out a copy of Ebony magazine and handed it to me, saying, "I know you have been dating a lot of girls without finding a stable relationship. Why don't you look through this magazine and show me what your ideal girl looks like." I paged through the magazine for a couple of minutes before I came to an advertisement featuring the most gorgeous girl I had ever seen. The girl in the ad seemed to be speaking to me through her beautiful eyes. I tapped my finger on the page and said laughingly, "Here, mom, this is my ideal girl." Mother looked at the girl in the ad and said "That one?" I replied, "Yes, mom, that's the one."

Two weeks later, while at a nightclub in downtown Minneapolis, I ran into a friend named Nicky. After we chatted for a bit, she told me she had a friend she would like me to meet. She was sure we would get along because our personalities were so alike. "Wait right here," she said, "I'll go find her." When Nicky returned, I looked up and almost fainted when I saw the face of her friend, for it was the girl I had seen in the Ebony magazine. I figured it had to be fate or destiny. I asked her if she had been featured in an ad in Ebony, and she replied "Yes, that is me."

Nicky was right—from that day on, her friend and I were inseparable. The girl's name was Wendy. She was half African American and half Finnish, and it was a beautiful combination. Wendy was also the daughter of an urban high school basketball coach who I really enjoyed talking sports with. Wendy was not only a well-known model, but also a singer and actress. Our relationship seemed to be a dream come true. I found Wendy so very interesting because even with all her beauty she seemed to be searching for something more. Being with Wendy taught me that no matter what you appear to have on the surface or what superficial material wealth you may possess, the most valuable thing you can have in life is peace of mind.

Wendy and I dated for ten years, even though we had already realized after the first year of dating that we probably would never marry. Our egos kept us together for a very long time. Wendy introduced me to the movers and shakers of the Twin Cities, and I really enjoyed the excitement of the nightlife. Wendy also provided emotional support when I lost two of the most important people in my life—my grandparents. Many days I just felt so alone, and I wished I had taken more time to learn all the knowledge that my grandparents had to give.

One evening as I slept, my grandfather came to me in a dream. In his normal way of speaking, he said to me, "Boy, it is time to move on with your life." I knew exactly what he meant, and it was that dream that gave me closure with my grandparents. I began to view my life differently and started realizing my purpose. At that time, I started taking the first steps toward a new goal:

teaching others about diversity.

Chapter Thirteen
New Directions

In late 1986, while I was visiting Wendy's great-grandmother's home, something small captured my attention. It was an unusual candy dish that depicted an African American woman looking up towards the sky. The dish was so interesting I questioned Wendy's family about it, but no one knew the history of the dish. I had no idea at the time, but that small dish would eventually set me off in a new direction. From that day on, I started researching and exploring similar types of black memorabilia to start my own personal collection.

I started finding black memorabilia in the most unexpected places. Some of the first artifacts I found were Aunt Jemima and Uncle Moses salt and pepper shakers. I found them at a flea market near Beloit, my childhood hometown, and when I purchased the shakers I wanted my grandparents to be the first to see them, hoping that they could give me some insight about these types of artifacts. But when I showed them the shakers, they didn't want to look at them. I asked them if they had seen stuff like this before and they said they had, but they also pointed out that black people were not the ones owning the black memorabilia. These items were owned by whites and represented white stereotypes of black people. I think that for this reason, the black memorabilia really made my grandparents feel sad, and it reminded them of a negative time in their past.

After I saw the reaction from my grandparents, I realized there was power in these artifacts. They represented concrete evidence of a body of history and racist attitudes toward black people in America. I had always been interested in African American history and in educating people, and it occurred to me that I could use these types of artifacts to teach others about diversity. As I continued to research and explore and search for more black memorabilia, the hobby starting filling a void in my life. Although I still missed the competition and excitement of basketball, the hunt for new objects to add to my collection occupied my mind. Every time I found an item of black memorabilia I would analyze the era it came from and imagine my grandparents and parents during the era. Some of the items even dated back to the era of my grandfather's grandmother, who was a slave in Mississippi.

When I first moved to Minnesota I lived on the St. Paul side of the Twin Cities, but after meeting Wendy I moved to downtown Minneapolis. I loved the energy I felt while living in the heart of the city, and Wendy loved it because of her modeling and singing career. In 1989, we decided to move out to the suburbs of Minneapolis to a city called Minnetonka. We moved into an apartment complex called the Cliffs. It was a great community and allowed easy access to downtown Minneapolis, but hated the commute to work every day, which on a perfect day was a 45-minute drive.

As I continued my research and exploration, Wendy had started pursuing a recording contract and her modeling career was going well also. She would often be gone to Los Angeles or New York in hopes of landing her big deal. I really did not mind because, as I mentioned earlier, we knew marriage would never happen for the two of us. In fact, I started to think I would probably be a bachelor for the rest of my life. I had always wanted to be a father and be there to raise my children with a committed and loving wife, but I really questioned whether it was ever going to happen.

From 1986 to 1996 Wendy and I played boyfriend and girlfriend, until I finally decided that I wanted something more out of a relationship: a family. I knew Wendy wanted to pursue her dreams in other cities, and in 1996 we decided to part ways. I was not hurt, but felt a burden had been lifted off my shoulders. Wendy was what I always wanted physically, but she didn't meet my needs emotionally. I started to realize it was the little things that count in a relationship, and the little things just weren't adding up with us. I knew I would miss Wendy's family who had accepted me as one of their own, but I had to do what was best for me.

Chapter Fourteen

Amy

While Wendy and I were living at the Cliffs in Minnetonka, two young ladies moved in next door. The young ladies were friends from Osceola, Wisconsin. One of them was more outgoing than the other, and I would have frequent conversations with her. The other one was friendly, but quiet. That was Amy.

The two ladies only lived in their apartment for about a year, but I would continue to see them every once in awhile at an event or nightclub in downtown Minneapolis. After Wendy and I broke up I started dating a lot, once again dating many women from different cultures. I was not meeting that special person that I felt I could share the rest of my life with. One night, I was out with my cousin Bryan at a restaurant when I saw Amy again. She was with a gentleman friend, but suggested we get together sometime for a drink. We exchanged numbers and said our goodbyes. I called her later that week, but she seemed very distracted. I figured she wasn't really interested, so I threw her number away.

As luck would have it, I ran into Amy again about three months later in downtown Minneapolis. She was with a group of friends and family celebrating a birthday. We started talking, and out of curiosity, I asked her why she had been so short on the phone when I called her. She explained that I had called her work number and her boss was standing near her. "Why didn't you call back?" she asked. I told her I had lost her phone number. We exchanged numbers once again and she gave me her home number to call.

The next time I called, she said she could not meet because she had a date with a past boyfriend she had recently broken up with. "Here we go again," I thought, "she's putting me off for a second time." I made up my mind to forget about her, but I couldn't help feeling disappointed. Amy was different. Something about her eyes and her character really captured my attention and emotions. There seemed to be something more to her that interested me.

About a week later, on the day before Labor Day, 1996, I was at a barbecue at my cousin Bryan's when Amy called. I invited her to come on over, and an hour later she was there. My cousin Bryan was used to me bringing many lady friends over to his home, so this was not surprising to him. But I found from that evening on that Amy was quite different from every other woman I had dated. She seemed to represent a combination of the very best qualities I had found in other women, all in one package. There were two things I loved about Amy from the very beginning. First and foremost, she was a friend. I felt so comfortable with Amy, it was almost like we were just pals hanging out together watching sporting events and sharing stories about life. Secondly, she was an extremely thoughtful person. She did all of the little things that can easily be taken for granted.

At first, Amy and I would get together about twice a week. I continued to date sporadically, but I found hanging out with Amy to be more enjoyable than spending time with anyone else. Eventually we started seeing each other more frequently, and she had the opportunity to meet my parents about two months after that Labor Day weekend date. My parents really enjoyed Amy. I can remember my mother commenting on how she enjoyed hearing Amy laugh.

At this point, it seemed that my relationship with Amy was perfect— but as we all know, in real life nothing is perfect. We had one problem, and that was her father. Amy was white, and although she had dated men of color as well as white men prior to our meeting, her father had not been able to accept the idea of her becoming serious with an African American man. "Why couldn't you date a white guy?" he asked her. "What if you had a child by an African American guy? Think how hard that would be on you and the kids."

These kinds of comments were things I had heard all my life, but not this close to my own front door. I was falling in love with Amy, and I couldn't just brush the hurtful comments aside.

I ignored the problem of Amy's father for quite a while in the beginning of our relationship, but after a year I could do it no more. I came out and told Amy that if our relationship was to continue, I had to meet her father and confront him about his biases and ignorance. Amy became very quiet, almost frightened. As I persisted, she began crying and said she had to go for a walk and talk to God. At last, she agreed to set up a meeting with her father.

Her father agreed to meet, and Amy was very nervous. I myself was neither nervous nor intimidated by this meeting because all of my life journeys with my family, schools, and professional career had prepared me for this very moment. What really kept going through my head was what my grandfather always taught me about not fearing any man, for they put on their pants the same way you do. When I walked into Amy's parents' home, I felt proud and confident about who and what I was. I only felt bad for Amy having to endure the fear of the unknown. I also felt proud of her because despite her fears, she had put her foot down and insisted that the meeting take place.

When I met Amy's father, I addressed him as "Mr." and respectfully introduced myself. We started talking about computers, as I knew this was his area of expertise. Thirty minutes into our conversation, I felt racial boundaries had faded for the moment. I really believe her father saw me as an individual and not an African American. As for Amy's mother, she was very religious and spiritual like my own mother, and we had an immediate positive connection.

The meeting with Amy's family was a big step for me, as it allowed me to continue to invest my emotions and feelings into our relationship. I think the meeting allowed Amy and I to fall deeper in love without having to worry about racial issues. Amy's father truly made an effort to understand me as a man, and he realized that I wanted what was best for his daughter, for as much as I loved Amy at that time I was willing to say goodbye to her and our relationship if her father was not accepting. I had expressed to Amy that her father is blood and I never wanted to come between a father and a daughter. God had created a plan for Amy and I, and we just had to follow his plan.

Chapter Fifteen
Gains and Losses

In our dating years Amy and I only encountered minor problems being an interracial couple, or maybe we just blocked out negativity around us and focused our energy on one another. We did have one early encounter one Fourth of July evening in 1997. We were on our way home after a day in Stillwater when we were pulled over by a police officer in North St. Paul, a town not far from my offices at Merrick. The officer looked in the car at me, and then proceeded to the passenger side and asked Amy, "Are you okay, ma'am?" Surprised at the question, Amy responded, "Yes, I'm fine, why are you asking?"

The officer then glanced at me again, and Amy said, "This is my boyfriend; what is the problem?" Without answering, the officer asked to see her driver's license. Amy said, "I'm not driving, so why do you need to see my license?" I could tell Amy was getting angry, and we both knew what was going on. Racial profiling was very prevalent at the time, and it was clear the officer's only problem with us was that I was black and she was white. I decided to play it cool. "Sir, is this a moving violation?" I asked politely. "Why did you pull me over?"

The officer told both Amy and I to get out of the car because he wanted to search the vehicle. Once again I questioned him, "Is this a moving violation?" The officer told me to go to the back of the car. I was very embarrassed because this was in a community that I worked in. I hoped no one I knew would drive by and see my car being searched.

The officer searched the car, and thankfully I had some brochures from

Merrick in my glove compartment that I think the officer recognized, which reassured him that I belonged in the area. After looking at the brochures, he told us we were free to leave, but that he was going to confiscate the fireworks in my trunk, which were illegal at the time. Amy was furious and wanted to say more, but I urged her to just let it go.

I remembered the officer's name, however, so I kept the incident in the back of my mind. I never did go to the police station to file a grievance, although maybe I should have. Within a year after the incident, I was playing basketball after work at the community center near my office and guess what officer showed up and played basketball? Well, I won't bore you with details, but I showed that officer how the game of basketball was to be played. I remembered every detail of the vehicle stop as I was taking it to him on the court. Sweet revenge.

In the winter of 1998 while driving alone from a weekend trip in Beloit, I decided that Amy was the person I wanted to spend the rest of my life with and who I hoped would be the mother to my children. I thought about all my past relationships and remembered what I had learned from each of them. "It's the little things that count," I thought to myself, as I mentally reviewed every little thing that was so special about Amy. Amy embraced my collecting and searching for black memorabilia, accepted and loved my family, and took the risk of introducing me to her father when she probably wasn't quite ready at the time to do so. Race was never a factor in our relationship; we cared too much for one and other to be bothered by the ignorance of prejudice.

I proposed to Amy in March of 1999, and we were married on October first of that same year. The wedding was classic. We were married on a Friday night in a Lutheran church in Stillwater, MN. On one side of the church sat all of the African Americans; on the other side were all the whites. At the end of the wedding ceremony, the pastor commented that he'd heard a lot of Amens from the African American side of the church, but he had not heard a single one from the other side of the church where the whites were sitting.

Everyone—African Americans and whites both—laughed at his observation, which was all too true. However, despite the seemingly wide gap created by cultural differences, what I found in Amy was stability and common ground.

COMMON GROUND

There's A Place Where We Can Meet
There's A Place Where We Find Peace

There's A Place That's So Familiar
There's A Place That's One In A Million

There's A Place That's Very Protected
No One There Is Ever Neglected

Common Ground
Is Where I Want To Be
Love And Happiness
Is All You Ever See

Common Ground
Is So Very Real
Heart Felt Emotions
Is All You Will Feel

Everyone Needs A Common Ground
If You're Looking Then Come On Down

Common Ground
A Place You've Always Known
Reach Out And Grasp It
And Make It Your Own

Although superficially they may have seemed very different, my family and Amy's were actually quite similar. Her uncles and aunts displayed a lot of the same characteristics as my uncles and aunts. The wedding ceremony was one big happy family, the way we hoped it would be. "Everybody was somebody and Christ was all" flashes through my mind as I remember watching children from different ethnic backgrounds dancing and playing together after the wedding.

In 1999 Amy and I moved to Stillwater, a historic town on the banks of the St. Croix River which was predominantly white. I was familiar with Stillwater because I had often shopped in the local antique stores searching for pieces of black memorabilia. We loved the historic charm of the area, including our first home, which was built in 1877. Since we had decided we wanted children, I felt that I needed to get involved in the community. In 2000, I was appointed to the Stillwater Human Rights Commission and later I would become the chairperson for the same commission. I enjoyed the commission because it helped to deal with the politics of the community.

Amy and I were blessed with our first child, a girl, in 2001. We named her Francesca Farrie Carr in honor of my mother. My mother was so proud that Francesca carried her name. One year and one week from the birth of Francesca, my mother and best friend passed away. Amy and Francesca were my foundation to get me through the pain.

After the funeral, my brother Steve and I decided to get my father out of the house for a change of scenery, so we brought him up to Stillwater to spend the weekend with us. It was an early Sunday morning, and we all decided to go for a walk in the park, taking along our dog, Benton. Amy and I had been to the park numerous times, as it was near her parents' home. While walking on the path, we suddenly became aware that a City of Stillwater facilities truck was rapidly approaching. The vehicle was moving so fast that my father, who was a double amputee but still able to walk, was afraid he would be hit by the speeding truck.

Abruptly, the truck stopped near us and a city employee jumped out, exclaiming, "Hey, you can't walk that dog in this park!" I looked at the gentleman and pointed to a sign nearby. "Look," I said, "the sign says dogs are allowed in the park, and you must have your dog leashed and pick up any dog waste your dog leaves behind."

The city employee refused to hear what I was saying and repeated that my dog was not allowed in the park and that we all would need to leave. My father and brother were becoming visibly upset, so I asked the employee his name, then I asked to see his employee badge. It was by chance that just two weeks prior to this encounter I had been appointed the chairperson of the Stillwater Human Rights Commission, and I informed him of this fact. The employee became nervous and sped away over a small hill in the park.

Back at home, I called the council representative for my ward and filed a complaint with the police department, and the city council and police department moved into action to fix the situation immediately. The police officer even offered to get the city employee and have him apologize to my family and me, but I told him it wasn't necessary. I only felt sorry for my father, because not only was he mourning the death of his wife, he also had to experience this degrading behavior in the new community that I had moved into, after I had been telling him how great the community was. I knew my father was probably thinking once again, "the more things change, the more they stay the same."

I often wonder what would have happened if it had been some other person of color being approached in the park by the city employee—someone who did not have the resources I had to get justice. They probably would have had no choice but to suffer the abuse and leave the park. I'm sure this city employee could not overcome his bias when he saw three African American males and a beautiful blond walking in the park at 7:30 a.m. on a Sunday morning. I wanted this incident documented by the police department for future interactions with this person in case he ever approached a minority again in an unprofessional way, but the damage was done when I had to see the look on my father's face during this very uncomfortable and unfortunate incident.

Four months after my mother's death, my second daughter was born. When Gionna Marie arrived I was so excited to have my second child, but I was also sad that my mother was not there to hold her and get to know her. As for my father, he was very happy that I had another girl because he always wanted a daughter and never had one.

Father was very lonely and brokenhearted after the death of my mother, and decided he wanted to move out of the home that he had worked so hard to buy in the great neighborhood in Beloit in 1972, and build a new home for himself in 2003 on the east side. I think he felt a change of scenery would uplift him. While my father's house was being built, I invited him back to Stillwater to visit for a week in March of 2003. We had a great time talking about life and playing with my two daughters. He and Amy were great friends and they were always joking with one another. He was very excited about the house he was having built and would be moving into that coming September. During that March visit my father joked about the incident in the park and expressed that he still had one more good punch in him if he needed to use it. My father was concerned about the community and wanted to know that my family and I were all right. Dad moved into his new home in September of 2003 as planned, and Amy and I and the girls went to visit him and help him decorate his new home. After about two months, however, my father confessed that his new house was just not a home without my mother.

In January of 2004 I announced to my father that Amy and I were expecting our third child. Dad was happy for us, and said that he wished my mother were around to enjoy all the grandchildren. Eden was to be born in the month of June. Then one early May morning, my father and his best friend Gene went to breakfast in Janesville, Wisconsin. My father was in the process of building a deck in the back of his new home, and after breakfast, he asked Gene to drop him off at a building supply store while he went in to get some supplies. Gene waited in the car, and it seemed like it was taking awhile for my father to come out. Suddenly, he looked up and saw an ambulance speeding up to the front of the store.

With a sickening feeling in his heart, Gene hurried inside the store. It was my father the ambulance was rushing to get to. He had suffered a massive heart attack and they were trying to revive him. My father died that morning, and I felt that the last of my foundation had crumbled beneath me. I had lost my father just when I felt I needed him most. This was a very critical time in my life, and my father was advising me on many life-changing ventures. I was in the process of purchasing and becoming 50% owner of a transportation business, and was trying to decide if I wanted to leave my 18-year career at Merrick to pursue the venture. I had a new baby due within a few weeks, and on top of that I was dealing with major Human Rights Commission issues in the City of Stillwater. I put everything on hold to mourn for my beloved father.

On the afternoon of the day Dad died, I was at home preparing to depart to Beloit to meet my brother and plan the funeral. I was really hurting bad and crying uncontrollably when I looked to the east skyline and saw the most beautiful double rainbow. I felt that it was my mother and father letting me know that everything was fine and once again they were together.

My third daughter, Eden Loretta, was born just nine days after we buried my father. I completed the business deal and left Merrick with very mixed emotions because of all the love I had for the mentally challenged clients I had worked with for the last 18 years, However, in a way I did continue with my mission to help the community, as the new transportation business I was developing provided mobility to the elderly and disabled. The City of Stillwater issue worked out fine, but my confidant and father would no longer be there for me to talk to. In 2006, Amy and I had our fourth daughter, Carmen Lee. The middle name Lee represents the middle name of my father and other family members.

Chapter Sixteen
Legacy

As life goes on, all the stories that my grandparents and parents taught me are being told to my four daughters. My daughters watch videos and view pictures of their grandparents and great-grandparents to keep the spirit of their loved ones alive. I have been blessed to have a wonderful family, and I want to keep alive the loving family values that I was taught as a youth.

I have been blessed athletically over the years, for I have been inducted into three Hall of Fame Ceremonies for basketball. I was inducted into the University of Wisconsin Eau Claire Hall of Fame in 1997 and the City of Beloit Hall of Fame in 2001. All three ceremonies were a great honor to me, but the largest of all happened in September of 2006 and it was the first one that neither of my parents were able to attend. The event was in Madison, Wisconsin, and we all drove out together so our four daughters could see their daddy inducted into the Wisconsin State Coaches Association Basketball Hall of Fame. The award was prestigious because the association had a very long history, and at that time only 10 basketball players had been inducted. I mourned because I wished Mom and Dad were there to witness their baby boy being honored in this way.

On the evening prior to the ceremony, we went to dinner at my Aunt Jeanette's in Beloit. After dinner, as Amy and the children and I were driving to the ceremony in Madison, something spectacular happened. My oldest daughter, Francesca Farrie, was looking out of the window of the car, and suddenly she said, "Dad, look at that pretty rainbow!" I looked and there was that beautiful double rainbow that I had seen the day my dad passed away. I told Amy and my daughters that was Grandpa and Grandma Carr, letting us know they were with us and saying hello. Now every time my children see a double rainbow, they say "There's Grandpa and Grandma Carr!"

At the ceremony I found myself gazing out at my children, and started to realize how proud my parents must have felt while supporting all the struggles and achievements I experienced along the path to becoming a Hall of Fame basketball player in my home state. All the lessons from my grandparents and parents prepared me for my life accomplishments. I owe it all to the love and nurturing they gave me. A poor black family had traveled North during the Great Migration in search of new opportunities, and they'd had an offspring who accomplished something they never would have imagined. I accepted the award in my ancestors' honor.

The challenges and struggles in life will continue to arise, but I feel I am prepared and ready to meet any encounter that I will face. I brave the battle not alone, but armored with the support of my loved ones that have passed on but live through my spirit. After my father passed away I created a presentation titled "Lest We Forget" in honor of my ancestors' legacy. To see my parents and grandparents' picture on large screens at colleges and universities always makes me chuckle, for they never could have imagined they would be seen and their stories would be told to hundreds and thousands of people. I truly believe my life's mission is to continue to share my public speaking and black memorabilia collection to educate and make people aware of a time gone by but not forgotten.

I'm always amazed and intrigued by the information individuals are seeking after one of my presentations. It seems participants are so shocked by the memorabilia that I display that they will wait until the presentation is over to ask questions face to face. I have had individuals from all age groups talk to me, from students requesting information and advice on interracial dating to grandparents sharing stories of the black memorabilia they saw as a child but never really understood. Many educators have expressed to me on numerous occasions that they did not realize that these types of black memorabilia existed.

I remember one Sunday morning in Stillwater, I was setting up for a presentation at a church when one lady who I would guess was probably in her late 70s to early 80s approached the table where I was displaying some black memorabilia. She picked up a figurine of a black child and commented "What a cute little nigger." I smiled and chalked up the experience as generational ignorance. But I was very happy when, after my presentation was completed, that same lady apologized to me, saying, "I probably should not have used the word nigger while looking at your figurine." The lady went on to explain that growing up in Stillwater she had not been exposed to various cultures. She thanked me for my presentation and said she would become more aware of what she says.

Awareness: that is the main purpose of my presentations. I cannot change how a person may feel about people that are different than themselves, but I can help people become more aware and sensitive about diversity. I always tell people that I speak not only about the African American race, but about the human race. All of our ancestors, no matter what our cultural background, have faced challenges and struggles that had to be overcome.

I love exposing and talking about negative racial stereotypes in my collection that were displayed in our society in advertising, toys, and various commercial products. These images are lasting evidence of how our society helped to propagate racial indignities and racist ideology through consumer goods—for instance, a "Nigger Hair" tobacco can, a toy called "Alabama Coon Jigger," and of course probably the most popular and well-known of all, Aunt Jemima's Pancakes. These were the images that children and adults associated with being black. I have found that negative racial images were displayed not only in the South, but all over the United States. Many of the artifacts were created in America, Japan, Germany, and many other countries.

I really like to educate youth today as to what it must have been like to live during the times that these images were out in the open and displayed freely in a corner store or market. I express to minority youth that these were the images supposedly representing them, and encourage them to view these offensive stereotypes from the past as motivation to better themselves and take advantage of the education and other civil rights they are afforded today. I explain to these young people that many of their ancestors gave their own blood, sweat, and tears in order for them to have the opportunities they never had. I explain that education is not only their right, but also their privilege because of the inequities our ancestors had to face.

I have witnessed many of the old stereotypes amongst white high school and college students starting to die. One in general is the association with all blacks loving watermelon. In my generation and before me, there were many stereotypes in marketing and various popular media of blacks stealing and eating watermelon. But today, I would say that 95% of the time when I'm speaking at a predominantly white school, the students are confused about the watermelon depictions. The white students say they have never heard or were aware about the association of watermelon with African Americans. I'm always so glad to hear this, for it tells me that upcoming generations will not carry on that stereotype.

Another stereotype is that all blacks like chicken. When I give a presentation I will ask the crowd, "How many people in here like chicken?" I will then reply, "Well, I see more than black people in here raising their hands to say they like chicken."

I have many artifacts of black memorabilia. Probably one of the most reviled and misunderstood is the jockey boy lawn ornament. Once popular in American yards, the statue depicts a black boy in jockey's clothing, often holding a lantern or a metal ring for hitching a horse. In earlier days, the statuette was viewed as a status symbol for beautiful estates and storefronts for lighting and hitching posts throughout the South. My own mother hated the sight of the jockey boy, and told me that during childhood, she and her friends would destroy the statues.

The jockey boy is a viewed as one of the most racially offensive figures in the realm of black Americana, although if popular legend is to be believed, the original intent of the jockey boy was much to the contrary. According to legend, the story of the jockey boy goes back to the days of our first president, George Washington. As described in the Encyclopedia of Black Collectibles written by Dawn Reno, the jockey boy was based on a real-life person. The boy's name was Tom "Jocko" Graves, and his father was known as a great horse trainer during the Revolutionary War. Legend has it that during the war, when General Washington was preparing to launch a surprise attack on the British, he made plans to pick up a horse from the stable where Jocko's father worked. It was a dark and cold night, and General Washington was traveling by boat along the Delaware River, as we have seen depicted in the famous painting. Jocko's father told General Washington that his son would be standing at the entrance to a canal holding a lantern to indicate where he should dock his boat to get to the stable.

As the weather rapidly turned colder and snow began to fall, the General and his party were delayed, but Jocko stayed true to his post. When Washington finally reached the canal, it had become so cold that the boy, who was 12 years old, had frozen to death while still holding the lantern. President Washington was so moved by the boy's courage that he had a statue commissioned in Tom "Jocko" Graves' honor. Although this legend cannot be proved or disproved, it goes to show that many African or white Americans really don't know the significance of some of the racial images we see in our world today.

My journey of educating and awareness will continue to increase as I go forward. I will continue to add to my black memorabilia collection and continue to research information of a time gone by but not forgotten. I hope to leave a path and a legacy for my children to continue as they share my stories to their children some day. I really do feel that our lives are what we make of it. You have a choice to give up when adversity happens or a choice to deal with it, learn from it, and overcome it. I have chosen in life to face, deal, and overcome.

I was very fortunate in 2006 to be featured in a local news story by Boyd Hooper, an Emmy award-winning journalist. The story was about my collection of artifacts and how they relate to struggles of African Americans in the past. My family was also shown in the spot. I received many positive emails and phone calls after the story aired, which made me feel very good. However, I also received criticism—mostly from fellow African Americans. Their comments stated that they admired what I was collecting and speaking about, but took issue with the race of my wife. They asked how I could do what I do and be married out of my race. My response was that if you listen to the core message I share in my talks, you would understand that I look beyond the color of a person's skin and connect with the soul of a person. I married out of love—and love is not based on the color of one's skin. My wife is proud of who she is, as I am proud and strong in my values of being a confident African American man.

The objection to interracial marriage is just another example of racism. Although it is painful to have this sort of racism directed at me, I take it as yet another lesson to share with others. I really try to share with people to be careful of making these types of racist comments, for they can potentially impact a person's life in ways we cannot predict. We should never underestimate the power our words may have on others.

I want to share one last story regarding my family. In the summer of 2000, both my mother and father were hospitalized at the same time in Beloit, Wisconsin. My brother Steve was truly a saint and savior during this time, for he had taken time off from work to help assist my parents. Steve said after he had spent numerous hours in the hospital room, my parents both told him he needed to go outside and get some fresh air. Steve went out to the parking lot at Beloit Memorial Hospital and walked around. He must have looked as tense and worried as he felt, because a gentleman he did not know approached him and asked what was wrong. Steve explained that his parents were both hospitalized. The stranger then asked if could come to my parents' room to pray for them.

Steve is a very protective and private person, but for some reason he allowed this stranger to come to my parents' room, where he shared a powerful and soothing prayer. Only after the prayer was completed did he think to introduce himself and ask my parents and brother their names. Once introduced to them, the man then smiled quizzically and asked, "Are you the family of Tony Carr?"

This gentleman, who is now a minister, shared a story from his past. He said that one day as a youth he was very hungry and poor, and I took him to the store to get something to eat. The boy would hang around the baseball park and watch my team play baseball. After many practices that he would observe, I finally went up to him and introduced myself and began talking to him daily at the park throughout the summer of 1974. The gentleman said that the support I gave at a difficult time had helped him to have hope in humanity. After all the years that had gone by, that act of support had stuck with him. He said he did not understand what drew him to Steve and my family that day, but after finding out who they were, it made perfect sense.

My parents called me that evening and shared the story with me. I felt very proud because I did remember the man, and, I was happy that my parents could experience firsthand the legacy of their values being passed on. The incident is one of those magical moments when you realize that small kindnesses really do make a difference. And that is something I keep in mind every day. Small things we do change the world for the better, and

it is through these acts of love and generosity that "time bring about a change."

Printed in the USA
CPSIA information can be obtained
at www.ICGtesting.com
LVHW052101130923
757981LV00011B/947